One must never be entirely comfortable
the truth behind every great Jiu-Jitsu tea
improving his game and his knowledge o
otherwise is to settle. I salute you my fel
us, it's a must... Our students deserve th(
belonging to our tribe.

Fernando Pessoa, a great Brazilian writer once said ... "The value of things is not the time they last, but the intensity with which they occur. That is why there are unforgettable moments and unique people!"

Karel Pravec is among those unique people; lucky are those who learn under his tutelage.

> *Master Renzo Gracie*
> *6th degree BJJ Black Belt, MMA Pioneer, 2x ADCC World Champion & Grandson of BJJ Founder*

Karel is one of my favourite training partners. The insights in his book are excellent to learn many techniques for advanced martial artists.

> *Georges St. Pierre, 12 time UFC World Champion, one of the greatest MMA fighters of all time & BJJ Black Belt*

I've been training with Fox since I was a Blue Belt. His Jiu-Jitsu is pure efficiency and has been an instrumental part of the Tristar Gym curriculum. In his book, he not only teaches a variety of powerful techniques, but he also includes pool workouts/techniques. The pool workouts, in my opinion, hit three birds with one stone. 1st it's therapeutic, 2nd it increases your fitness level, and 3rd it makes your technique instinctual. Drilling is the key to success, but comes at a price: it taxes the body. Fox has found a brilliant solution.

> *Firas Zahabi, Renowned MMA Coach & BJJ Black Belt*

Back in the early 1990s, Karel was one of my first training partners in the early days of the Renzo Gracie Academy. We came up the ranks together and now that we are both long time Black Belts, I frequently ask him to visit my school to teach the professional class. I cannot say enough good things about his technique and teaching methods. I highly recommend the book!

> *Matt Serra, Former UFC World Champion, Decorated BJJ Black Belt & Renowned MMA Coach*

DEDICATION

To my wife & text editor Norma, my daughter Elissa, and my family

To my students and my training partners

To my instructors, especially Renzo Gracie & John Danaher

To my friends

Copyright © 2016 Karel Silver Fox Pravec
All rights reserved.

ISBN: 1523883936
ISBN 13: 9781523883936

Text Editing: Norma Pravec
Photography: Louis & Oriana Wesolowsky
Layout & Underwater Photography: Mike Gonzalez
Uke: Frank Roberts

FOREWORD

I feel distinctly honored to be asked to write the Foreword to Karel's book, mostly because I know the real Karel Pravec. The central premise in this remarkably well-conceived instructional manual is, of course, how a scrawny older practitioner can submit a younger fitter one. The real Karel is uniquely qualified to answer this topic. Not because he is older and scrawny. He most assuredly is neither. Thirty seconds on the mat with him, and trust to the fact, an entirely different set of adjectives come to mind. Karel Pravec's very existence, coupled by his success in the lion's den of high level Brazilian Jiu Jitsu, is a testament to an underdog cutting through his opponents.

You see, when Karel was a child, he watched in horror as Soviet tanks overran his country. His father, a well-respected high level diplomat, was black listed and persecuted by the Soviets. The real Karel, along with his family members, ultimately wound up in New York City, USA. The South Bronx part of the city, where souls are forgotten and none is the number. The real Karel fought his way out of a place where most abandon hope. The real Karel graduated from college in 3 years, and got a Master's degree in Finance from an Ivy League university. He asked for a free ride from no one. He did it the old fashioned way. He earned it. In a society enamored with the meretricious, Karel is the antithesis. The real Karel is a beacon of light, worthy of emulation.

Karel and I were among a small group of the original students of Renzo Gracie. The group grew larger, and most quit when things got edgy. Not the real Karel. Since I didn't quit either, I had a front row seat to the ascension of Karel Pravec to the very highest levels of technical excellence in Renzo Gracie Brazilian Jiu Jitsu and that very same level in the arena of life.

The real Karel Pravec is the embodiment of Coolidge's iconic quote:

Nothing in this world can take the place of persistence. Talent will not: nothing is more common than unsuccessful men with talent. Genius will not; unrewarded genius is almost a proverb. Education will not: the world is full of educated derelicts. Persistence and determination alone are omnipotent.

Wayne "Big Chuck" Bradshaw, Author of Jersey Tough

ABOUT THE AUTHOR:

Karel (Silver Fox) Pravec is a 3rd degree Black Belt under legendary Renzo Gracie with over 23 years of Brazilian Jiu-Jitsu experience (since 1993). During his training at the world renowned Renzo Gracie Academy, Karel has trained with and studied under some of the highest authorities in the art, including Renzo Gracie, John Danaher, Rodrigo Gracie, Daniel Gracie, Matt Serra, Nick Serra, Ricardo Almeida and Shawn Williams. Karel is a highly sought-after instructor who has taught seminars across the United States, Canada, Europe, and Latin America. He has coached BJJ and submission grappling on the national and international level (ADCC, IBJJF, GQ and NAGA tournaments) and cornered amateur & professional MMA fighters.

Karel has studied martial arts, including Tae Kwon Do (3rd degree black belt) for 30 years. Karel started studying martial arts in 1986 under Master Byung Sung Cha, reaching the rank of 3rd degree black belt in the World Tae Kwon Do Federation in 1995. In the early 1990s, while studying and teaching Tae Kwon Do, Karel expanded his martial arts knowledge by attending numerous seminars, including Muay Thai, Jeet Kun Do, and Gracie Jiu-Jitsu, and incorporated the techniques into his martial arts arsenal. Incorporating the various martial arts into one's training became known as mixed martial arts (MMA).

After attending the 1st seminar on the East Coast given by the Gracie family (Helio, Rorion, Rickson, Royce and others), Karel was convinced of the effectiveness of Brazilian Jiu-Jitsu, which was further confirmed by the style's success in the early mixed martial arts competitions. Karel started taking regular classes in Brazilian Jiu-Jitsu in the New York/New Jersey area when they first became available in 1993, when **Craig Kukuk**, the 1st American black belt in Brazilian Jiu-Jitsu, moved to the East Coast. Shortly after, Renzo Gracie, one of the most successful and dynamic practitioners and teachers of the art moved from Brazil to open an academy with classes in New York and New Jersey, and Karel became one of Renzo's first students.

Studying under **Renzo Gracie** and **John Danaher**, Karel achieved the prestigious rank of Renzo Gracie Jiu-Jitsu Black Belt in July 2006.

Although Karel competed infrequently, he demonstrated the success of his style (focus on submissions) by winning:

1st Place – 2006 Tenth Grapplers Quest West (Master Lightweight Division) – all matches won by submission

1st Place – 2007 NAGA World Championship (Advanced Director – Open Weight) – all matches won by submission, lightest competitor in the division

2nd Place – 2008 Grapplers Quest U.S. Nationals (Masters – Absolute) – lightest competitor in the division

3rd Place – 2008 Pan Am Championship No-Gi (Black Belt – ADULTS – Lightweight)

1st Place – 2010 European Championship (Black Belt – Absolute Division – Senior 3) and 2nd place in Lightweight division

Karel continued to compete at the highest level (World Championships - both Gi and No-Gi) in the adult divisions into his late 40's.

Karel has a Bachelor's degree from State University of New York (Albany) and Master's degree from Columbia University. The education and analytical skills have helped Karel continue growing both as a practitioner and teacher of Brazilian Jiu-Jitsu.

INDEX

For additional information on Karel, visit www.SilverFoxBJJ.com

For videos of the techniques and sequences described in this book, visit www.Digitsu.com (Discount Code: f12gh49)

To request a seminar at your academy, contact Karel at: karelpravec@optonline.net

Section	Pages
Introduction	1 - 2
Overview	3 - 6
Chapter 1 – Guillotine & Follow-ups	7 - 22
Chapter 2 – Omoplata & Follow-ups	23 - 36
Chapter 3 – Bolt Cutter Grips/Ude Gatame Attacks & Follow Ups	37 - 47
Chapter 4 – Bottom of Cross Side Attacks	48 - 60
Chapter 5 – Patterns/Commonalities Across Techniques	61 - 77
Chapter 6 – Solo Water Training	78 - 125
• Individual Techniques	80 – 99
• Combinations	100 - 125

This book is for educational purposes. The publisher and authors of this instructional book are not responsible in any manner whatsoever for any adverse effects arising directly or indirectly as a result of the information provided in this book. If not practiced safely and with caution, martial arts can be dangerous to you and to others. It is important to consult with a professional martial arts instructor before beginning training. It is also very important to consult a physician prior to training due to the nature of the techniques in this book.

INTRODUCTION

Many people have asked me to write a book about BJJ, but I always declined as I don't like to write. However, I was inspired to do this by the number of people training BJJ who asked a very similar question – "I'm turning whatever age (usually 30) and getting beaten up by younger, bigger, stronger, more athletic... guys. Am I too old for BJJ?" The short answer is "No". Some practitioners try to make up for their size, strength, age etc. deficit by more strength, intensity, speed etc. This leads to more injuries, disillusionment, and frequently quitting BJJ, but I believe there is a better way – setting up your opponent with technical attack and if he is able to defend the initial attack, follow up and catch him off his defense ("outfoxing" your opponent if you will).

I started BJJ at 29 in 1993 after training primarily striking martial arts for 7 years, but utilizing the techniques, sequences, and concepts presented in this book has allowed me to compete in the adult black belt divisions at the highest level (including Absolute Division; I usually walk around at 155-160 lbs.) through my 40s. At this point, in my early 50s, I still train every day – alternating soft/water training and training hard with elite practitioners significantly heavier and/or younger than me.

The key to "outfoxing" your opponent (i.e. the strategies of Fluid BJJ) are:

- Impeccable technique
- Recognition of opportunities for follow up (Triggers)
- Maintenance of momentum (Follow-up technique)

I believe water drilling (Chapter 6) has been instrumental in my ability to train 7 days/week while continuing to improve my skill set through:

- Mental (imagery) rehearsal which allows me to physically build up muscle memory and perfect technique while technically having an "easy" day
- Repetition (drilling) that does not severely tax my body
- Water qualities which improve overall fitness and lower the gravity or training partner's pressure on my joints

This book is geared toward a skilled BJJ practitioner who wants to submit a skilled and stronger opponent through technique, leverage and "outfoxing" rather than power and strength, and focuses on technical attacks and maintenance of the momentum. These concepts can be applied to any style of BJJ.

It will augment the conventional BJJ wisdom held by many practitioners of position before submission. I will argue (especially in submission grappling context where "punishment" for inferior position is not as severe as in MMA/self-defense context) that MOMENTUM can be more important that position. This is evidenced in tournaments where a competitor is submitted when he refuses to give up a position and winds up giving up too much momentum to his opponent. The key to maintaining momentum is to watch the sometimes subtle changes in your position relative to changes in your opponent's position (= TRIGGERS), and react to them on your terms rather than on the opponent's terms.

OVERVIEW

BJJ may not be intuitive, but it is logical. It relies on structural leverage and efficiency of movement. There are times when you make an error (technical, timing, etc.) in your attack or your opponent properly counters you with his timing, strength, etc. (= TRIGGER). During this time, you have a limited opportunity to follow up with another submission or sweep attack. Unless your error was too great, generally speaking, your opponent's defensive reaction is predictable. Seeing the Trigger in time and promptly acting upon the momentum allows a smaller, weaker, older, etc. practitioner to prevail (more human chess than a war for position).

The Trigger is the moment when your opponent takes away your leverage, structural superiority, element of surprise, etc. At that point, you are faced with a choice:

- Continue with the original attack, and rely on strength and/or speed

OR

- Take advantage of your opponent's defense and regain leverage, and/or element of surprise, i.e. recognize the Trigger and Counter his Counter with an appropriate technique before he nullifies your attack (= Fluid BJJ)

This approach can be applied to any type/style of BJJ game.

Why "fluid":

- Minimize injuries
- Outsmart/outmaneuver the opponent (BJJ = human chess)
- Goes with original concept of BJJ for a smaller/weaker person to defeat a larger/stronger opponent
- Suited for practitioners going against a skilled opponent who has knowledge of BJJ/grappling

- BJJ is not just a physical pursuit, but also a martial art with strong mental and character components
- Reality is that a skilled opponent most likely will counter your move; staying one step ahead keeps the fight on your terms
- Keep the momentum of the attack, which is very valuable in combat

Basic Principles:

- Submission driven (submit opponent or obtain superior position if he defends), but be aware of possible striking (i.e. in a self-defense or MMA context)
- Fluid - Transitions create openings/opportunities
- Utilize the opponent's reaction against him (knowing his possible options, but limiting his movement)
- Follow up on an unsuccessful 1st or 2nd attack to keep momentum on your side (i.e. he is defending, rather than attacking)
- Shouldn't just be a cat-and-mouse game chasing your opponent; as you follow up, the follow-up attacks should tighten the noose and the submission should occur by the 2nd, 3rd, or 4th technique
- These techniques do not require:
    - ✗ Athleticism
    - ✗ Extreme flexibility
    - ✗ Inordinate amount of strength

    But with:

    - ✓ Technique
    - ✓ Precision
    - ✓ Momentum

    Anyone should be able to utilize them.

- Can be applied to any aspect/style of BJJ, and you can create your own follow-up combinations based on your game. Perfect the attacks and defenses specific to your game, and as your partners wise up to them – they start to counter/escape by usually establishing a pattern → follow up with an attack off their counter

Keys:

- Must be technical (i.e. precise)
- Fluid – dictate change of position, do NOT let opponent dictate (= be 1 step ahead)
- Elicit reaction/set up your opponent. From top, keep pressuring him or go for a submission; if you get reversed → you must have his arm, neck, or leg tied up so you can submit him or re-sweep. From bottom → you look to sweep or submit your opponent.
- Transitions create openings/opportunities
- Utilize leverage and/or 2 limbs on 1 limb attacks, etc.
- If possible, attack 2 fronts at once
- All of the above = wind up limiting the opponent's options

Drilling:

The attack and follow-ups have to be:

- Discovered through trial and error (look for consistency in the opponent's defense to your attacks)
- Then DRILLED to perfection
- And finally applied

Drilling can be an under-rated part of training for some BJJ practitioners, but it is an absolutely necessary part of BJJ which helps you incorporate and then perfect new elements/techniques into your game. I particularly believe in solo water drilling to help me continually grow my game. Practicing these movements in the water, with its buoyancy and resistance, has resulted in more effortless and fluid movement on the mats.

Illustrations/Examples Series:

NOTE: The sequences and techniques in this book below do not necessarily encompass all of the possible attacks or follow-ups/scenarios, but are the most efficient counters to the most common defenses. In all photos, when I refer to myself, I'm wearing the white gi (opponent is in the blue gi).

CHAPTER 1 – GUILLOTINE & FOLLOW-UPS

Guillotine is one of my favorite weapons, and is the technique that got me the nickname, Silver Fox. Younger, stronger and more athletic guys would come in for a double leg take-down, I would push their head to the outside, and they would be tapping as soon as we hit the mats. I consider it one of the classic BJJ techniques, albeit underutilized by many practitioners. It is highly effective against opponents who are larger or stronger with better wrestling skills. One of the highlighted points in this chapter is body positioning which typically gets less emphasis than the various grips. I believe that grips are more of a personal preference (mine is the more traditional grip – ½ of my hand on my wrist and ½ on my choking hand), and play a lesser role in guillotine effectiveness than body positioning and the shoulder rolled forward.

Utilizing the principles of Fluid BJJ (follow-up attacks) and Head Control, I usually submit my opponent or wind up in a strong top of side control position. Basic principles of the guillotine are:

- Offensive use - Guillotine guard pass, Head snap down, Opponent turtles
- Defensive use – from opponent's single or double leg take down
- "Head control" concept (will submit opponent OR wind up on top)
- Proper body positioning (more on your side rather than on your back) is the key
- Follow-ups (anaconda, pin, one handed guillotine etc.)
- Make sure the OPPOSITE LEG of your choking arm is preventing your opponent from getting his body on the opposite side of his head (i.e. if you are choking with your left arm, your right leg must be over his body and vice versa)
- Shoulder MUST BE rolled forward (in the middle of your opponent's shoulder blades) to prevent his head from popping out

Guillotine Application – Offensive (Standing)

Get your inside grips.

Snap opponent's head down.

Turn your body to the right to fence his head in between your upper torso and your arms.

Roll your left shoulder forward. Make sure opponent's head cannot pop out.

Hips forward, and right leg ready to make sure it goes over your opponent's back as he takes you down.

Guillotine Application – Offensive: Open Guard

Opponent playing open guard.

Step in (one foot between opponent's legs).

As opponent sits up to react to your guard pass, snap his head down.

Roll your left shoulder forward & turn your body to your right so his head is isolated by your body and cannot pop out. This position makes it difficult for your opponent to take your back.

Flatten him out with your hips. At this point you can pass his guard as he is flat on his back.

Once you pass his guard, guillotine choke him (if his hands are defending your guard pass, you can choke him from half guard; once he starts protecting his neck, pass his guard and return to the choke).

Guillotine Application – Opponent Turtles

I like attacking opponent's turtle from North/South position as this makes it very difficult for him to roll and create a scramble to escape.

Drive into him DIAGONALLY (if he doesn't push back, it is very easy for you to take very strong top of cross side position – I've done this to skilled opponents 100 lbs heavier than me). This opens his neck if he pushes back (great majority of the time).

As he pushes back, to prevent him going backwards, his neck elongates – i.e. opens. This is your cue (trigger) to fold underneath him (using windshield wiper movement of your legs). Again, make sure your left shoulder is ROLLED FORWARD!

As you land on YOUR SIDE, apply the choke. Notice my body position, when the choke is on. This position will result in:

- Strong carotid choke
- Your ability to sweep him in case choke fails

Guillotine Application - Details

I prefer traditional grip (half of my hand on my wrist, half on my hand). There are other grips (high elbow, 10 finger, pretzel etc.) – you can experiment as to which one is best for you, but you can apply the principles below to all of them.

Keep your left hand high up on your chest. Tuck in your elbow. Remember – as in all chokes, we are trying to make the hole as small as possible.

Roll your left shoulder forward. This is a key part of a good guillotine – it prevents your opponent's head from popping out and allows you to follow up, which results in him being submitted or swept.

Turn your body diagonally so your left ribs isolate his head. Again, this prevents your opponent from freeing his head (if that happens, that is the worst failure of your guillotine).

Guillotine Follow-ups - Anaconda

Attack guillotine by pushing (diagonally) into your opponent.

When he drives back to try to stay on top, fold underneath him.

Your inside leg prevents him from jumping over and allows you to adjust your angle in case he tries to square up to you (alignment of his body with yours allows him to defend the guillotine).

As he tripods (gets his hips high) to protect his neck, his center of gravity gets high and he's easily knocked over with your inside (in this case left) leg. NOTE: Some opponents will flop on their side to get a step ahead but will wind up in same position (below).

He successfully defended guillotine, but your efficient follow-up will utilize his defense against him. Keep tight grip on his neck with the choking arm (left in this case) and stay on your side to prevent him from freeing his head and scrambling up.

Pass you right arm over the top of his left arm that attempts to block your hips from coming up – if he doesn't, it's easy for you to get on top (see below), grab your right bicep with left hand, anchor your right hand on his left lat, and choke (RNC style).

Stay on your side so your body movement towards him pushes his head deeper into the choke. Bring your elbows together and through his chest – like a Rear Naked Choke. As in all chokes, try to make the hole as small as possible.

Anaconda Squeeze Detail

Grab your bicep.

Elbows together.

Through his chest.

Guillotine Fail to One Handed Choke

Trigger: This time, your opponent doesn't block your hips.

Get an underhook (in this case, your right arm underhooks his left arm).

Underhook at his elbow gives you stronger leverage than at his shoulder.

Arch, so his head gets under your body (otherwise, it will block you from turning towards him).

Turn towards him to get strong top of side control. As you are turning, adjust your choking hand (in this case left) to make it go 1) deeper and 2) flat and closed like a flipper. See below for details.

Once you've turned, your hand is trapped by your body, so it's important you make the hand adjustment before you land on top. Once on top, COMPRESS your arm down with your chest to achieve a strong carotid choke.

One Handed Choke Detail

Hand flat and high up on your chest.	
Before you land on top of cross side, sink it deeper than the guillotine grip you had before.	
Bring your chest down on the choke to create compression for a carotid choke (basis of all chokes) rather than pulling on his head (this is more of a neck twist that some people don't tap on).	

Anaconda Fail to Re-Guillotine

Trigger - opponent is very strong and keeps your anaconda (RNC type) grip loose (by opening up your elbows).

"Allow" him to come back towards you to re-guillotine him. The keys to this are:

- Shrimp away to keep a good angle
- Make sure your shoulder rolls forward so his head cannot pop out

Re-guillotine.

Notice my body position:

- On my side
- Left shoulder rolled forward
- Right leg over his back (choking with left arm)
- Left leg on his hip (ankle flexed) for additional control

Anaconda to Mounted Guillotine

Trigger - opponent is very strong and keeps your anaconda grip loose (by opening up your elbows with his arms).

Post on your shoulders as you roll over on your opponent into mount.

As you land mounted, adjust hand grips.

In this case, your back is more flat on the ground (if you were on your side, re-guillotine may be a better option).

You may need to adjust your body to make sure your hands are properly wrapped around his neck. Apply compression pressure & finish!

Guillotine Reinforcement – Closed Fist Choke

Sometimes, either you or your opponent's body position is such that you don't have the best angle for the carotid choke.

Some examples are listed below.

In such cases, we can reinforce the grip with a closed fist on the open carotid.

Example of imperfect body position for guillotine – weak mount.

Example of imperfect body position for guillotine – he's moving towards you and you need to re-guillotine, but you didn't properly adjust your body angle.

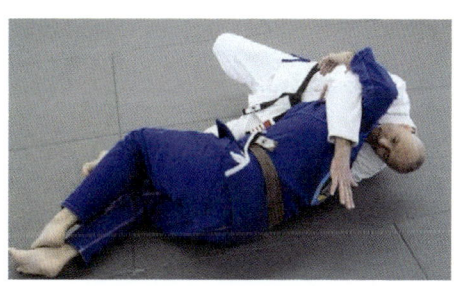

As he's coming on top, you try to re-guillotine and you didn't shrimp far enough.

Notice that as you didn't shrimp far enough, your body is too aligned with his. This makes for a weak guillotine, and the probability of freeing his head increases. Especially so, when he's pulling down on the wrist of your choking arm.

In such case, switch your right hand grip from your own wrist to putting your right fist on his open (left) carotid.

You can reinforce the pressure of your right fist by wedging your right elbow against your right hip so the pressure comes from your body drive rather than just pure arm strength.

CHAPTER 2 – OMOPLATA & FOLLOW-UPS

Omoplata (shoulder lock utilizing your legs) has become one of my favorite attacks. Most BJJ practitioners tend to view omoplata as a weaker submission relative to the triangle or armlock from the guard. This is rightly so, as omoplata has more and easier escapes than the other 2 major guard submissions (triangle and armlock). However, as the opponent also knows this, if he gets in trouble, he is most likely to offer you an omoplata as he feels more confident to escape. As such, you will have more opportunities to attack with an omoplata, and developing strong follow-ups will significantly improve your game.

Omoplata – Start with Short Armlock

This position is frequently defended by your opponent putting himself into an omoplata to escape. From that point on, he's on the run, therefore he's not passing your guard or striking you.

Make sure your opponent's hands are off your chest, then trap his left wrist under your armpit. Your left foot is on his hip.

Lay back (thereby stretching his left arm), while keeping his hips away with your foot on his hip.

Keep his head between your knees, your right foot on his hip (or upper thigh) and arch your hips to the ceiling for a quick submission.

Omoplata to Inverted Armlock

If your opponent anticipated your movement from above (Short Armlock), this is a good follow-up attack.

Trigger – he defends by turning his body away (but his arm is straight – if bent, see below). Straighten out your left leg and turn your body to the left (rotating on LEFT SHOULDER – do not posture up on your elbow).

As you rotate, bring your right shin on the back of his neck if he keeps his head on the ground (do NOT bring your right leg over his head) and continue turning to your right.

Stop on your side facing his feet.

Grab his closer pants leg (or ankle) to prevent him from helicoptering over your body, and arch your hips into his arm for an inverted arm lock finish.

Omoplata

This time, as you try to apply the short arm lock, your opponent turned his body AND bent his arm (= Trigger that you cannot go for an inverted arm lock).

By turning away and bending his arm, he protected himself against short or inverted arm lock, but his arm is still isolated and his body is turned – great opportunity to attack omoplata.

Bring your right leg over his arm (and keep it heavy = inner thigh pushes down towards the floor).

Keep your thighs together so he cannot pull his arm out.

Sit up quickly. You can get momentum by pendulum swinging your outside leg (in this case, left leg) but you must keep your right leg tightly bent to prevent his arm from escaping.

Bring your right calf close to his left elbow to increase leverage (by moving your hips a bit further away and back from your opponent).

Finish omoplata. Don't forget to seat belt grip his back and sit up while keeping his shoulder and elbow pinned to the floor.

Omoplata Follow-up – Back Take & RNC

As you attack omoplata, your opponent anticipates it early.

Trigger: Opponent sharply turns his body away (to limp arm free his arm) while your hips are still facing away from him.

Make a big swing away with your right leg to his opposite hip.

And get the 2nd hook (with your left leg) while bringing your head closer to his.

Pull him back by his shoulders.

And finish with a strong Rear Naked Choke (RNC).

Elbows together and through his chest.

Ear to ear (= better choke and control).

Omoplata Follow-up – Arm Triangle

Attack omoplata.

As you try to sit up, opponent rolls very quickly.

Trigger: As your opponent's hips start to clear your right arm = you are losing the omoplata finish.

Disengage your right arm, and slide forward on your right knee.

Use your head to trap his right arm while using your left arm for base.

Slide your right arm deep (your right forearm should be flat against the floor) around opponent's neck.

Use your body to drive forward to elongate his neck.

Connect palm to palm, with your forearm flat against the floor (this grip has stronger choking power than the RNC type grip sometimes used).

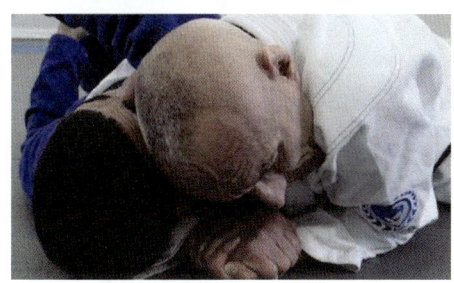

Flatten your own body against the floor.

Roll your right shoulder forward, bring your hips flat to the mat and finish the submission. NOTE: Use your head actively to push against opponent's left arm.

Omoplata Follow-up - Mangledome

Trigger for this Follow-Up: opponent posts his right arm to protect his neck as he goes for a powerful roll to escape your omoplata (hoping that he'll put you in his guard).

Underhook his right (far) arm with your right arm.

Feed his right arm to your left hand.

Grab his right wrist with your left hand (your left thumb is facing down).

Pump his arm down forcefully.

This pressure pins his shoulders to the mat, and forces him to go into a tight roll over his shoulders rather than a wide roll that he was hoping for. Continue holding his right wrist with your left hand.

As he finishes his roll, his own body traps his right arm (while you still hold his right wrist with your left hand).

Pin his left arm by flaring out your right shin (frequently you can get a bicep slicer off this). Your right arm goes under opponent's neck.

As his body is prone, his neck is wide open. Roll your right shoulder forward to cause a carotid choke. This position is also a great form of control without much power on your part.

Omoplata Enhancement – Modified Toe Hold

You attack omplata.

Your opponent awaits your move to keep his escape options open.

Reach your right hand over his Achilles heel = that will be your fulcrum for the toe hold break).

Reinforce your grip with your left hand.

Drive his toes to his buttocks for a submission.

Omoplata Follow-up – Bicep Slicer

Omoplata attack.

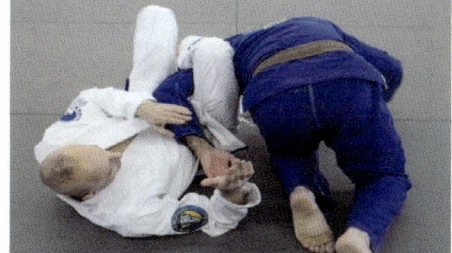

Trigger: Opponent rolls very quickly before you have a chance to sit up and seat belt grip him. Lean back far to make sure his feet clear your body completely (otherwise, he can use any light grip to square up to you to put you in his guard).

Use your left hand to guide his left ankle away from you (this prevents the really flexible types to put you in their guard) as you flare out your right shin to pin his left bicep/elbow.

Your shin should be parallel to your opponent's body.

Shift your right shin back (still parallel to his torso) while moving your torso above his, causing the bicep slicer. You can get a quick submission and/or very effective form of top side control.

Omoplata Follow-up – Sweep

Trigger: Your opponent initiates his roll before you sit up or you sit up and his buttocks pass under your right arm = you lost the omoplata submission. Rather than holding on and most likely being put in his guard, use your attack as a sweep and go for a superior position.

Lean back far enough so his feet clear your torso, and guide his left ankle away with your left hand.

Windshield wiper your feet away.

Swing your upper body over his torso.

Establish very strong top of cross side.

CHAPTER 3 – BOLT CUTTER GRIPS/UDE GATAME ATTACKS & FOLLOW-UPS

The bolt cutter grip is one of my favorite ways to attack from open guard. I use it as a sort of opening salvo when I attack from the open guard. It can be used on a standing or kneeling opponent. The key to this attack is to make your opponent flare out his elbows just a bit. This can be accomplished through off-balancing him or actually pulling his elbows out in a circular movement and forward.

I like it for the following reasons:

- The 2 on 1 attack allows you to straighten out even a very strong opponent's arm
- The bolt cutter grip provides additional leverage
- Your isolation of the opponent's arm generally forces him to turn away (i.e. makes it less likely to be struck by him in a self-defense scenario) and also allows for numerous follow-ups
- It also allows for a smooth (and relatively low risk) transition from closed guard to open guard

Your head gripping and controlling your opponent's wrist is the key component of this technique, and once you get good at it, this attack and follow-ups work like a charm.

Ude Gatame/Upside Down Armlock

Sit up to isolate your opponent's arm (in this case, his right arm).

Your left hand weaves under his armpit and over his shoulder. Note how I am using my head as another limb to prevent him from pulling his arm out or swimming it in.

Get the bolt cutter grip = palm to palm (no thumbs). Continue using your head.

Bring your right elbow down and left elbow up as you start to pull away to stretch out your opponent's arm.

Catch his forearm with your head by leaning towards your left.

Lean back to stretch his arm out and control his arm with your head as you let his arm slide down and his wrist gets caught by your head and shoulder.

Adjust your grip to RNC like grip (your left elbow bent, on top of his right elbow, reinforced by your right arm) and pressure down for the submission. Note how my body is bowed out to allow for breaking room, and my head & neck (your left ear to your left shoulder & twist your chin to your right – like holding a phone) are heavily engaged in controlling his arm.

Upside Down Armlock Follow-up - Triangle

You attack bolt cutter, but your opponent reacts quickly or you make a mistake in your grip.

Trigger: He pushes forward and swims his right elbow in and starts turning it down (i.e. he escaped the upside down armlock). Pin his elbow to your chest as you lay down and get your right foot off his hip and over his shoulder.

Swing your right leg over your opponent's neck to set up a triangle.

Finish strong triangle submission.

Upside Down Armlock Follow-up – Inverted Triangle

Attack bolt cutter.

Before you have a chance to stretch out opponent's arm, he buries it under his body.

Bring your right leg to the same side to add leverage, but he grips his gi.

Weave your left foot under opponent's body to the opposite side (make sure your opponent's left arm is trapped by your calf).

Swing your right leg over his neck

Lock up an inverted triangle. Note that I'm on my side and my left hand holds his right pants leg (or ankle) to prevent him from going north/south to defend the triangle. Squeeze your inner thighs for an efficient finish.

Upside Down Armlock Follow-up – Rolling Armlock

Opponent is standing. Attack bolt cutter/ude gatame.

As you bring your right leg over to reinforce, opponent's posture starts to break. Notice that your opponent's right arm is bent which together with his posture broken makes it difficult for him to just rip his arm out.

Opponent postures on his free hand and attempts to roll out of the arm lock.

As he rolls, adjust your legs so when he lands, he winds up in a traditional top of cross side arm lock.

Keep your legs heavy (toes down) and thighs together for a tight submission.

Upside Down Armlock Follow-up - Guillotine

This follow-up is against a particularly strong opponent. Attack bolt cutter/ude gatame.

Opponent buries his arm and grabs his gi. Bring your right leg over his body to increase your leverage. You realize opponent is very strong and it will be hard to dislodge his arm.

Swing your right leg wide back to opponent's other side.

Swinging your leg wide will give you momentum to windshield-wiper your leg out of the way and your head comes up above his.

Your right hand snaps his head down.

Lock up your guillotine grip.

Fold under your opponent for a guillotine choke.

Finish the guillotine.

Upside Down Armlock Follow-up – Reversal

This follow-up is also against a particularly strong opponent. Attack bolt cutter/ude gatame. It is very similar to the one above (Guillotine follow-up).

Opponent buries his arm and grabs his gi. Bring your right leg over his body to increase your leverage. You realize opponent is very strong and it will be hard to dislodge his arm.

Swing your right leg wide back to opponent's other side.

Your swinging leg will give you momentum to windshield-wiper your leg out of the way and your head comes up above his.

Your right hand snaps his head down.

This time, your opponent fears the guillotine submission and backs away, giving you the reversal.

Opponent is reversed and you get ready to pass his guard (knee slice pass is very good for this position).

CHAPTER 4 – BOTTOM OF CROSS SIDE ATTACKS

The caveat of this chapter is – learn escapes from bottom of side control. Bottom of cross side is generally considered an inferior position that should be escaped. Ironically, you are probably less likely to be hit if you're on the bottom of cross side (the second your opponent postures up to strike you, regain guard) than from your opponent being inside a sloppy guard; however, attacks from the bottom of cross side could be good ways to reverse the momentum. Even in the event of failure of these attacks, you generally accomplish putting your opponent in your guard, thereby improving your position.

I have gotten many submissions utilizing these attacks. As your opponent blocks your escapes (generally moving his arms and/or hips in a predictable pattern), this opens up an opportunity for you to catch him with one of the following techniques.

Bottom of Cross Side Armlock

Your opponent is on top with traditional arm position (left arm under your head, right elbow by your hips).

Bump up high.

As your hips drop (your frame briefly keeps him off you), slide your buttocks closer to your heels.

Bring your left leg up over his head and right shin across his body.

- Pinch your thighs
- Your right ankle is flexed so he cannot pull his arm out
- Your left heel over his head comes close to your buttocks to prevent him from gaining posture

Arch for a tight finish (Note: his wrist is under your armpit for better leverage).

Bottom of Cross Side – Inverted Triangle

Opponent is passing your open guard.

As he pushes your leg out of the way, he controls your left leg with his right arm to prevent you from shrimping.

As he drops in, he temporarily leaves his right arm between your legs.

Bump sideways, turn to your right hip and push his head down towards your legs. Swing your left leg over his head.

Pinch your thighs together to prevent him from extracting his head and arm.

Turn completely to your right hip and lock up an inverted triangle.

Grab his pants leg (ankle in no-gi) to prevent him from going North/South, and squeeze your thighs together for the finish. You can also reinforce the finish by body locking his torso with your arms (your head up by his left hip to prevent him from circling).

Inverted Triangle Attacks (Kimura)

If you feel that your angle is off, your legs are too short, or your opponent has a strong neck and you start to lose confidence in your inverted triangle, grip his left wrist with your right hand.

Weave your left hand to your right wrist to lock up a kimura grip.

Pull his hand away from his body and above his back, and finish with an inverted triangle/kimura combination. Keep the inverted triangle as dual submission/form of control.

Inverted Triangle Attacks (Keylock)

Trigger: Your opponent reaches for your knee to strip off the inverted triangle.

Grab his left wrist with your left hand. Keep the inverted triangle as dual submission/form of control.

Connect your right hand to your left wrist for a key lock/Americana grip and push his wrist up for a very strong finish (Note: This will kick in quickly as your inverted triangle prevents your opponent to go with the pain).

Inverted Triangle Attacks (Toe Hold)

Trigger: Your opponent starts to move North/South to defend the inverted triangle.

Stop him before he steps over your head by grabbing his left foot with your right hand, and weave your left hand under his shin to grab your right wrist.

Keep the inverted triangle as dual submission/form of control.

Finish the toe hold submission by driving his foot towards his buttocks while using your left forearm as a fulcrum for the break.

Inverted Triangle Attacks (Sweep)

If you feel that your angle is off, your legs are too short, or your opponent has a strong neck and you start to lose confidence in your inverted triangle, you can use this position/head grip for a sweep.

Trigger: Your opponent steps over your head into North/South position to strip off your inverted triangle.

Keep your triangle tight and rock your opponent towards his head and turn to your left as he loses his balance.

Finish your reversal.

Establish strong top of cross side control.

Bottom of Cross Side – Leg Keylock

Your opponent grabs your left pants leg with his right hand.

He stretches your leg out to prevent you from applying inverted triangle.

Trap his right arm with your right leg (make sure your Achilles tendon is above his elbow).

Swing your left leg out and bend it.

Your right ankle goes under his right wrist.

If necessary, keep your left leg near to help push his arm into position.

Keep your right leg bent.

Lift your ankle up in a Keylock/Americana motion to finish with your right leg.

Bottom of Knee on Belly – Kneebar

Your open guard gets breached.

Opponent leg drags you.

And puts his knee on your belly.

Bump him forward with your inside (right) leg.

As he puts his hands on the ground to regain his base, start inverting underneath him.

Spin to your right, pushing off his outside (left) leg with your hands while your left leg is going inside his leg, and your right leg wraps around his right leg on the outside.

Thrust your hips up to make sure your hips are above his knee.

Clamp down on his right ankle with your armpit.

Straighten out his leg and pinch your thighs.

Finish with a strong knee bar.

CHAPTER 5 – PATTERNS/COMMONALITIES ACROSS TECHNIQUES

There are many commonalities among different BJJ techniques (for example, the way you roll your shoulder forward in a guillotine, or the shoulder of your arm under the opponent's head rolling forward when you are on top of cross side, applying an arm triangle etc.). Seeking and understanding these patterns, and drilling one of them will help you hone your technique for the other scenarios. You need to have an awareness of these commonalities so you can apply them across techniques to make your training more efficient.

For illustration purposes, the following commonalities are shown:

A. Windshield-Wiper Scenarios – moving your legs in a windshield-wiper movement helps you set up attacks, reversals and/or defenses.
B. Shoulder Rolling Forward – as discussed above, this movement is present in many different attacks and/or pressure scenarios.
C. Underhook Scenarios – getting an underhook on your opponent allows you to better control your opponent so you can improve your position or attack for a submission.

A. Windshield-Wiper Scenarios – Same Side Armlock

The opponent has an underhook by your left hip (if his right arm is on the left side of your torso - see next page on how you can set up this arm placement).

Windshield-wiper your left leg parallel to your opponent's torso. Note: Your left knee should be on the level of his hips, but your left shin is about 6-10 inches from your opponent's body so your leg can come up when you apply the arm lock.

Your left leg steps over his head. As you start to fall back into the arm lock, swing your upper body in a circular motion (in this case to your right) until you get perpendicular to your opponent.

Keeping the sole of your left foot flat on the ground (this makes your leg heavy over his head), bring up your right shin. The break is the scissor action between your right leg pushing left, and your upper body pushing right. Note his wrist is in your right armpit.

A. Windshield-Wiper Scenarios – Same Side Armlock

This is the same attack (from previous page) where the opponent's right hand starts out on the left side of your torso. Circle to your left towards North/South and switch your arms from the traditional top of cross side.

Your opponent will very often try to get an underhook on your right side (as he's thinking of escaping that way).

Pressure his left arm to make it appear that you're attacking that arm, thus making him unconcerned about his right arm. Do NOT grip his right arm tightly. It's hard for him to extract his right arm from your right leg and torso positioning.

Swing your left leg over his head.

Notice how his right wrist is under your right armpit, effectively trapping his arm between your right upper thigh and your torso.

Sit into the armlock position in a circular motion (in this case clockwise) keeping his right arm straight and right wrist pinned under your right armpit. Sole of your left foot stays on the ground to make that leg "heavy".

The break is the scissor action between your right leg pushing left and your torso pushing right. You can reinforce your leg with your hands.

A. Windshield-Wiper Scenarios (De La Riva Reversal)

Opponent standing in your De La Riva guard.

Push his left thigh with your right foot to stretch him out.

He pushes your right foot off his thigh to step over it.

Windshield-wiper your legs to your left to get them out of your way and to generate forward motion of your torso.

As you sit up, your head goes on the inside to avoid being guillotined.

Drive off your left foot (while keeping his leg trapped with the bend of your right leg).

Finish the reversal.

A. Windshield-Wiper Scenarios (Guillotine)

Your opponent is turtled.

Drive diagonally into him.

As he pushes back, connect the guillotine grip so you don't have to adjust it as you get into position.

Windshield wiper your legs towards your opponent (counter clockwise) to make your "fall" into guillotine smooth. You don't want to jump underneath him as this makes you overshoot your target. Pull him by his neck like a yoke.

Place your legs in proper position (see Guillotine Chapter for additional details) and finish the guillotine.

A. Windshield-Wiper Scenarios – Leg Lock Battle

Opponent attacks your legs.

Swim your feet in a circular motion to free them.

Then swim both of your feet inside his legs to protect them.

Lift with one of your hooks under opponent's knee (in this case, your right foot) while windshield-wipering your left foot back.

Swing your right foot back in a windshield wiper motion, again generating forward movement with your torso.

With the top position accomplished, start passing his guard.

B. Shoulder Rolled Forward – Top of Cross Side

Rolling your shoulder forward scenarios.

Traditional top of cross side, with your left arm under your opponent's head. Drive your left hand deeper (under opponent's left shoulder blade), keeping your palm open and facing the ceiling.

Tilt your body to your left & roll your shoulder forward to generate tremendous pressure on your opponent's neck – with the right placement, this generates strangle pressure on his right carotid which can result in submission.

B. Shoulder Rolled Forward – Guillotine

Set up guillotine – note the opponent's head isolation. The set-up includes rolling your shoulder forward to 1) Prevent his head from popping out and 2) <u>Keep it rolled forward throughout the entire guillotine attack.</u>

Fold under your opponent. Keep your shoulder rolled forward.

Finish the guillotine.

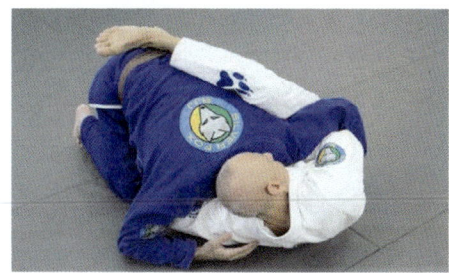

B. Shoulder Rolled Forward – Upside Down Armlock

Sit up in open guard.

Attack with the bolt cutter.

Roll your left shoulder forward to "fence in" your opponent's arm tightly and have his right wrist swing towards your neck, where it gets trapped. For the finish, etc. – see Upside Down Armlock Chapter.

B. Shoulder Rolled Forward – Arm Triangle

This finish is available from passing the guard, from the mount, following up on a failed omoplata etc. Swim your right arm under opponent's neck with his right arm isolated between his head and your head.

Get your right arm deep (your right forearm should be flush with the floor).

Bring your head down, connect palm to palm, and roll your shoulder forward to generate pressure on the carotids. For additional details – refer to Omoplata (to Arm Triangle) Section.

Shoulder rolled forward - detail.

C. Underhook Scenarios – Knee Cut Pass

Sliding through opponent's guard with your right knee, it is imperative that you get the underhook on his left arm with your right arm to prevent him from taking your back.

As you finish your pass, the underhook helps pin his shoulder to the mat.

Good head control will pin the opponent and give you a good position for further attacks.

C. Underhook Scenarios – Anaconda Fail – Come Up

We try for anaconda follow-up.

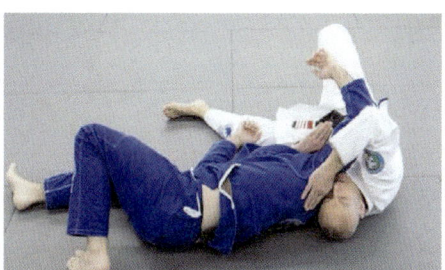

Opponent is keeping his elbow very wide (you can either fight to compress it with your leg, or get an underhook & wind up on top).

Get an underhook to prevent your opponent from turning towards you.

Arch (to allow his head to go under your body) and turn to your left.

Wind up in top position with one-handed guillotine submission.

Or finish in a strong top of cross side position.

C. Underhook Scenarios – Upside Down Armlock

Strong underhook (with shoulder rolled forward) is the starting point for the upside down armlock attack.

Stretch out his arm.

Adjust your grip.

Finish upside down armlock. For additional details, refer to Upside Down Armlock Section.

CHAPTER 6 – SOLO WATER DRILLING

Disclaimer – Do these drills in a safe environment under the supervision of a lifeguard. I have hit my head on the bottom of the pool in one instance and couldn't figure out which way was up or down.

Benefits of solo water drilling:

- Water resistance in all directions builds speed and fluidity.
- Nature of solo drilling makes you aware of your own movement to make sure it is precise (rather than simultaneously paying attention to your own movement and your opponent's movement). This is particularly important when first incorporating new techniques, and helps with muscle memory.
- Since you are performing drills without a partner, it forces you to visualize your opponent's movement, and therefore you can start expecting his movement on the mats.
- You can drill any technique (later on we go over some examples of techniques/sequences).
- Active recovery - water buoyancy lightens the load on your joints and back, allowing you to train more often.
- Longevity – it is not as intense as a "lively" rolling session, yet it is another day of training.

Many of the drills discussed below are described in greater detail in earlier chapters. If you have a hard time visualizing your own or your opponent's movement, it is important to remember that you can create any drills, combinations, or sequences to improve your game. They can be simple or complex. The buoyancy of the water allows you to drill techniques you may know but want to perfect, or experiment with and develop new and unpredictable movements. When your partners catch on to them, you can develop further counters and/or follow ups. As long as you try to keep your movement technical, precise, and crisp, executing your visualization and water properties can significantly enhance your game.

The techniques are broken down into two Sections:

A) Individual technique drills to get started in water training
B) Combinations / Sequences drilling

In any drill, pay particular attention to the critical parts of each technique. The critical parts are pointed out in this section, or you can refer back to a specific technique on the mats in the previous chapters.

A) Leg Trip

Take a fairly narrow stance.

Pull your opponent on you.

Right knee to the floor.

Sweep your right heel back.

Drive your hips forward.

Finish the take down.

A) Seoi Otoshi

Get an underhook with your right arm.

Grab your opponent's right wrist with your left hand.

Pull him forward.

Load him up on your hips.

Back step with your left leg.

Your right leg goes across your opponent's right shin.

Pull his right arm while pulling him forward with your underhook.

Finish the take down.

A) Head Snap to Guillotine

Snap your opponent's head down with your right hand towards your left hand (choking arm).

Make sure his head is past your lat muscle.

Wrap his head with your left arm (Note: Your body tilts to trap his head).

Roll your shoulder forward, hand up high on your chest, and your body coiled for maximum strangulation.

Fold underneath your opponent to finish the submission.

A) Arm Drag to Guillotine

Arm drag your opponent's right arm to the left side of your body.

As your opponent resists the arm drag by pulling back, use your opponent's momentum (and windshield wiper your legs) to rise up.

Snap your opponent's head down.

Wrap the guillotine grip.

Tighten up your grip.

Coil for the finish. Notice the leg and body positioning as well as the smallest hole possible for the opponent's neck.

A) Armlock Drill

Open your legs and spin to get the proper angle on your opponent (in your guard).

Pivot to your left. Keep his left wrist pinned to your chest. Bring your left foot up your opponent's back.

Keep your opponent's posture broken by keeping your left foot tight and heel low.

Bring your right leg over your opponent's head.

Bring both heels down and arch for the finish.

A) Jumping Armlock from Top of Cross Side

As you pass your opponent's guard, he's pushing you with his closer (right) arm.

Reach for his right wrist with your right forearm.

Throw your hips forward.

Bring your left hand in to reinforce your grip on his wrist and bring your left leg over the opponent's head.

Pin his wrist to your chest and start leaning back.

Arch for a tight armlock finish.

A) Top of Cross Side Armlock (Far Side)

As you are passing your opponent's guard, he starts turning on his right side towards you.

Slow down his turn by bulldozing him with your chest.

Your right arm reaches for his left arm and brings him fully on his side (Note: Your right forearm blocks him from turning all the way to his knees).

Put your torso on his arm and over his torso, so he cannot move his arm.

Post your left hand on the ground close to his left hip so you have a smooth entry.

Leave your right leg over his head.

Get a good grip with both of your arms over his left wrist, and lean back smoothly into an armlock position.

Arch for a strong submission.

A) Triangle Drills

Open your legs to attack triangle.

Swim (no pun intended) your left foot out to clear his arm.

Lock up a triangle. Notice my right hand on my left shin – this buys you time to lock up the proper angle by keeping the opponent's posture broken.

Tighten your legs (thighs together).

Triangle the other side (same sequence as above, just the other leg).

Swim your right foot to clear the opponent's arm.

Lock up your right ankle under your left knee. Notice my left hand on my right shin – this buys you time to lock up the proper angle by keeping the opponent's posture broken.

Tighten your legs (thighs together) to finish.

A) Omoplata

Pull your opponent's left arm. His wrist should be next to your body (on the right side of your ribs).

Pivot your body to the left.

Keep your legs tight so he cannot pull out his arm.

Sit up, seat belt grip.

Finish omoplata.

A) Knee Cut Guard Pass

Slide your knee through your opponent's legs.

Make sure you get a strong underhook with your right arm.

Your head should be either next to his head or on his left shoulder to keep his mobility limited.

Get a strong top of cross side.

Hips down, and pull up on your opponent's right arm.

A) Over/Under Guard Pass

As you try to pass his guard, he blocks you with his arms stiff.

Switch to an Over/Under grip on your opponent's legs (in this case your right arm is under his left leg and your left arm over your opponent's right leg).

Kick out your right leg to clear his guard.

And start moving to the top of your opponent's cross side.

Switch your right arm to underhook his left arm to keep him pinned.

Move up higher on his torso.

And pin him for a strong top of cross side.

A) Windshield Wiper Movement

Sit up in your guard.

Get your feet off the ground.

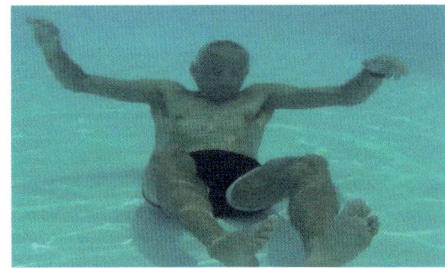

Sweep your feet back in a windshield wiper movement.

Generate up and forward momentum of your torso.

Sweep you heels back.

Drive forward for the reversal.

B) Triangle to Omoplata

Set up a triangle.

Your opponent breaks to his left to defend the triangle.

Open your legs and pivot to switch to omoplata (on his right arm).

Keep your left leg deeply bent so he cannot pull his arm out.

Get the seat belt grip and sit up.

Finish omoplata.

B) Omoplata to Arm Triangle

Pivot to attack omoplata (on your opponent's left arm). Notice that the pivot is always done curled up to minimize friction with the ground.

Bring your right heel tight to prevent your opponent from freeing his arm.

As you attempt to sit up,

Open your legs.

Knee cut slide to clear your opponent's legs.

Reach your right arm wide to trap his head and right arm.

Connect palm to palm.

Square up your body to the floor.

Roll your shoulder forward and finish the arm triangle.

B) Omoplata to Inverted Armlock

Pull your opponent's left arm to attack omoplata.

He turns to his right to escape the omoplata, but leaves his arm extended.

Roll up on your left shoulder to attack inverted arm lock (Notice my right shin is on the back of opponent's neck as he keeps his head down).

Keep turning until you are on your right side, facing his feet.

Arch into a finish.

B) Hip Heist to Triangle

Your opponent is sitting on his knees in your guard, not willing to engage.

Hip heist to roll him over.

As he drives you back to the mats,

Swim your right foot from under his left arm, and bring it over his head.

Finish the triangle.

B) Hip Heist to Guillotine

Your opponent is sitting on his knees in your guard, not willing to engage.

Hip heist.

As he drives you back into the mat,

Wrap your left arm over his head.

Shift your hips to your right before you land.

Finish a tight guillotine.

B) Guillotine to Single Hand Guillotine

Attack with the guillotine.

Your opponent flops on his right side to defend.

Get an underhook with your right arm, arch, and turn to get on top of cross side.

Adjust your hand flat, fingers together for a single hand guillotine.

Flatten your opponent down with your chest to achieve maximum compression.

B) Guillotine to Anaconda

Attack with the guillotine.

Your opponent flops on his side (or you knock him over) to defend.

Swim your arm over his left arm & connect for an anaconda grip.

Grab your bicep and anchor your right hand on his lat.

Squeeze your elbows together.

Stay on your side and walk towards your opponent to make the choke stronger.

B) Guillotine to Anaconda to Mounted Guillotine

Attack with the guillotine.

Your opponent flops on his side, and you switch to the anaconda.

If he keeps his elbow wide to prevent you from locking up a solid anaconda grip, roll up on your shoulders (your body is lined up with your opponent).

Bring your legs over your body.

Roll up over your left shoulder.

Into mounted position & mounted guillotine.

Squeeze (Notice the reinforcement with my right fist on the opponent's left carotid).

B) Knee Cut Guard Pass to Guillotine

Knee cut guard pass (to your left / your opponent's right side).

Your opponent gets an underhook on you.

Turn towards him with your left shoulder rolled forward.

As he comes up on top of you, wrap his head with your left arm.

Lock up your guillotine.

Finish the guillotine (shoulder rolled forward, your hand high up on your chest and your elbow swept back).

B) Knee Cut Guard Pass to Kimura

Knee cut guard pass
(to your left /your opponent's right side).

As you pass his hip line, your right underhook is marginal and he starts to turn towards you.

Grip his left wrist with your right hand.

Your left arm comes over the top of his left elbow.

Connect kimura grip (make a figure 4 with your right hand on his left wrist and your left hand connecting to your right wrist).

Step your left leg over his head to get the angle and room to torque his arm.
Notice the angle of my hips to generate most leverage.

B) Knee Cut Guard Pass to Knee Bar

Attempt knee cut guard pass (to your left, your opponent's right side)

Opponent blocks the guard pass, back step over his left leg.

Back step needs to be high so your opponent does not hook your left leg and attempts to take your back.

Grab his left heel.

Pin his leg with your arms and under your head, and extend for a knee bar.

B) Turtle Step Back to Back Take

Your opponent turtles well and you can't get the guillotine grip.

Post your hand on his upper back.

Back step your right leg over his back towards his upper right thigh.

Bring your left foot back so you are straddling his lower back.

Pull him diagonally backwards.

Put your hooks in as he opens up and finish with the Rear Naked Choke.

B) Ashi Garami Sweep & Get Up

Grip the back of your opponent's knees.

Pull him forward (or yourself in).

Open your legs for an ashi garami position.

Raise your hips up and into him to knock him over.

As your opponent starts to lose balance,

Start windshield wiper movement.	
Sweep your legs back.	
Finish the sweep & start passing his guard.	

B) Strip off Ashi Garami to Rolling Omoplata

Opponent ashi garami's your right leg.

Keep your right foot solid on the ground, strip his left foot off your hip, and keep turning to your right to keep the bottom of your right foot flush with the mat.

Lift up your left foot and slide your right foot deeper under the opponent's left arm.

Initiate the roll.

Roll over your right shoulder.

The momentum will lift his torso off the mat.

Keep your right leg bent so he cannot extract his arm.

Seat belt grip over your opponent's lower back (or your right hand goes under the opponent's right/far elbow) for better control.

Finish a strong omoplata.

B) Armlock to Omoplata to Rear Naked Choke

Pin your opponent's arm.

Pivot for an armlock.

As your opponent pulls the attacked (left) arm out,

Pivot more for an omoplata (on your opponent's right arm).

As your opponent turns away hard to defend the omoplata attack,

Before your hips get to a position to lock him up (facing towards him), he turns away sharply to escape the coming omoplata.

Sit up and reach for his neck.

Wrap your right arm around his neck.

Connect with your left hand (palm to palm).

Choke your opponent with a modified Rear Naked Choke (palm to palm).

Printed in Great Britain
by Amazon